JUL   2009

D1611891

First Biographies

Wilma Rudolph

by Eric Braun

Consulting Editor: Gail Saunders-Smith, PhD
Consultant: Billie Luisi-Potts, Executive Director
National Women's Hall of Fame
Seneca Falls, New York

Capstone press
Mankato, Minnesota

Pebble Books are published by Capstone Press,
151 Good Counsel Drive, P.O. Box 669, Mankato, Minnesota 56002.
www.capstonepress.com

1 2 3 4 5 6 10 09 08 07 06 05

Library of Congress Cataloging-in-Publication Data
Braun, Eric, 1971–
    Wilma Rudolph / by Eric Braun.
    p. cm.—(Pebble books. First biographies)
    Includes bibliographical references and index.
    ISBN 0-7368-4234-9 (hardcover)
    1. Rudolph, Wilma, 1940—Juvenile literature. 2. Runners (Sports)—United
States—Biography—Juvenile literature. 3. Women runners—United States—
Biography—Juvenile literature. I. Title. II. Series: First biographies (Mankato, Minn.)
GV1061.15.R83B73 2006
796.42'092—dc22   2004029074

Summary: Simple text and photographs introduce the life of Wilma Rudolph, an
Olympic runner, who overcame childhood illnesses to become the first American
woman to win three gold medals at the Olympics.

Note to Parents and Teachers

The First Biographies set supports national history standards
for units on people and culture. This book describes and illustrates
the life of Wilma Rudolph. The images support early readers in
understanding the text. The repetition of words and phrases helps
early readers learn new words. This book also introduces early
readers to subject-specific vocabulary words, which are defined in
the Glossary section. Early readers may need assistance to read
some words and to use the Table of Contents, Glossary, Read More,
Internet Sites, and Index sections of the book.

Table of Contents

Time Line

1940
born

early 1940s
gets sick with
scarlet fever
and polio

Growing Up

Wilma Rudolph was born in Clarksville, Tennessee, in 1940. As a young child, she was sick with scarlet fever and polio.

Wilma's hometown, Clarksville, Tennessee, in the early 1940s

Time Line

1940
born

early 1940s
gets sick with
scarlet fever
and polio

6

Wilma lost the use of her left leg. She went to the hospital. She had to wear a leg brace. Doctors said she might not walk again.

◄ Meharry Medical School in Tennessee, the hospital where Wilma went

Time Line

1940
born

early 1940s
gets sick with
scarlet fever
and polio

1950
learns to walk
without a
leg brace

Wilma worked hard
to get better. Her family
helped her. She visited
a doctor twice a week.
By age 10, Wilma could
walk without a leg brace.

◀ Wilma (right) with her older sister, Yvonne

Time Line

1940
born

early 1940s
gets sick with
scarlet fever
and polio

1950
learns to walk
without a
leg brace

1956
runs in the Olympics
in Australia; wins a
bronze medal

Olympic Athlete

By age 16, Wilma was a track star. She ran in the 1956 Olympics. She won a bronze medal.

◀ Wilma (second from left) with her Olympic teammates

Time Line

1940 born	**early 1940s** gets sick with scarlet fever and polio	**1950** learns to walk without a leg brace	**1956** runs in the Olympics in Australia; wins a bronze medal

Wilma practiced hard.
She wanted to do better
in the next Olympics.
In 1960, she ran in the
Olympic Games in Italy.

1960
runs in the Olympics
in Italy

Time Line

1940	early 1940s	1950	1956
born	gets sick with scarlet fever and polio	learns to walk without a leg brace	runs in the Olympics in Australia; wins a bronze medal

Wilma won three gold medals. She was the first American woman ever to win three gold medals at the Olympic Games.

1960
runs in the Olympics
in Italy; wins three
gold medals

Time Line

1940
born

early 1940s
gets sick with
scarlet fever
and polio

1950
learns to walk
without a
leg brace

1956
runs in the Olympics
in Australia; wins a
bronze medal

People were proud of her. Wilma's hometown held a parade. Many people came to cheer for her.

1960
runs in the Olympics
in Italy; wins three
gold medals

Time Line

| 1940 born | early 1940s gets sick with scarlet fever and polio | 1950 learns to walk without a leg brace | 1956 runs in the Olympics in Australia; wins a bronze medal |

Later Years

Wilma graduated from college in 1963. She later married and had four children. Wilma became a teacher and a track coach.

1960
runs in the Olympics in Italy; wins three gold medals

1963
graduates from college

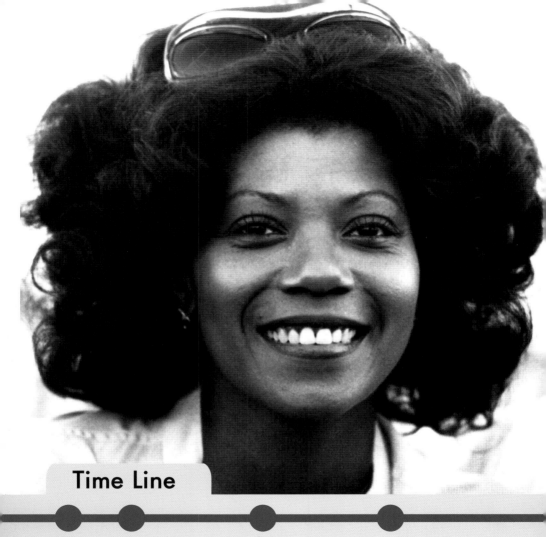

Time Line

| 1940 born | early 1940s gets sick with scarlet fever and polio | 1950 learns to walk without a leg brace | 1956 runs in the Olympics in Australia; wins a bronze medal |

In 1981, Wilma started a group to help young athletes. She taught them to work hard like she did. Wilma died in 1994. People remember her as a hero.

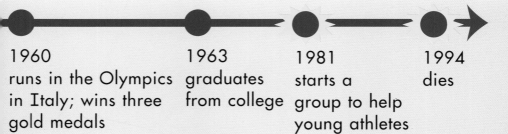

1960
runs in the Olympics in Italy; wins three gold medals

1963
graduates from college

1981
starts a group to help young athletes

1994
dies

Glossary

athlete—a person trained in a sport or game

leg brace—something worn on the leg to support it

medal—a piece of metal shaped like a coin that an athlete receives for winning an event

Olympic Games—a competition of many sports events held every four years in a different country; people from around the world compete against each other.

polio—a disease that attacks the nerves, spinal cord, and brain

scarlet fever—a disease that causes a bright red rash, a sore throat, and a high fever

track—a sport that includes running and jumping in different events; track is also called track and field.

Read More

Conrad, David. *Stick to It: The Story of Wilma Rudolph.* Spyglass Books. Minneapolis: Compass Point Books, 2002.

Sherrow, Victoria. *Wilma Rudolph.* On My Own Biography. Minneapolis: Carolrhoda Books, 2000.

Internet Sites

FactHound offers a safe, fun way to find Internet sites related to this book. All of the sites on FactHound have been researched by our staff.

Here's how:

1. Visit *www.facthound.com*
2. Type in this special code **0736842349** for age-appropriate sites. Or enter a search word related to this book for a more general search.
3. Click on the **Fetch It** button.

FactHound will fetch the best sites for you!

Index

Word Count: 204
Grades: 1–2
Early-Intervention Level: 16

Editorial Credits
Katy Kudela, editor; Heather Kindseth, set designer; Patrick D. Dentinger, book designer;
    Kelly Garvin, photo researcher/photo editor

Photo Credits
AP/Wide World Photos, cover, 8, 10, 20
Corbis/Bettmann, 4 (inset), 14, 18
Getty Images Inc./Time Life Pictures/Ed Clark, 6; George Silk, 1, 16; Mark Kauffman, 12
Photo courtesy of Billyfrank Morrison, 4